W9-BIC-906

PLUS COLORING!
Ages 3 and Up

Halloween
Cut & Paste
WORKBOOK FOR PRESCHOOL

What picture comes next?

    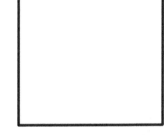

Match the heads to bodies!

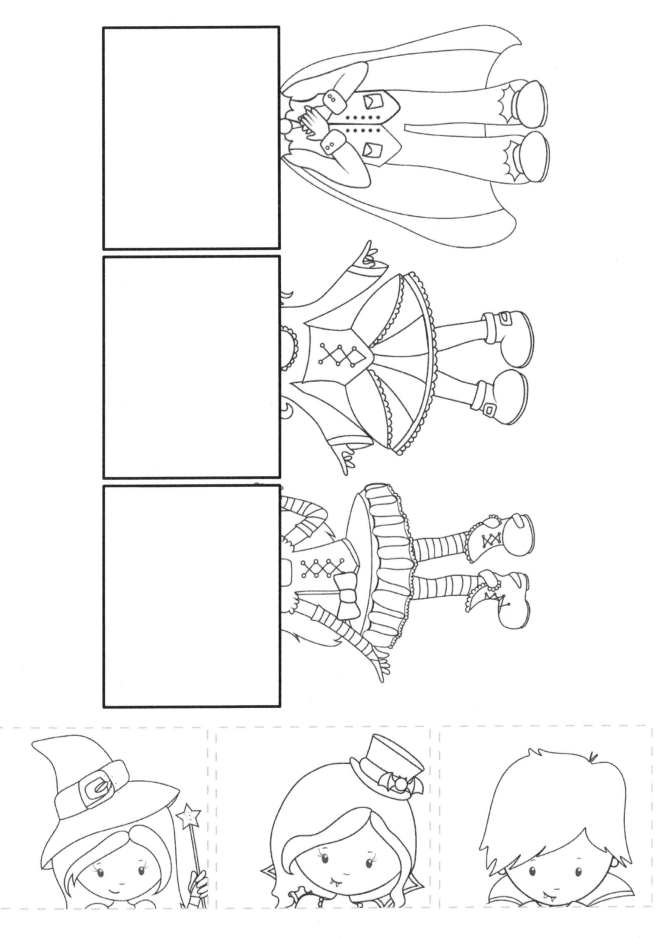

Put a face on the pumpkin!

What will the ghost look like?

What picture comes next?

Put the pumpkin
puzzle back together!

What will the vampire look like?

What will Frankenstein look like?

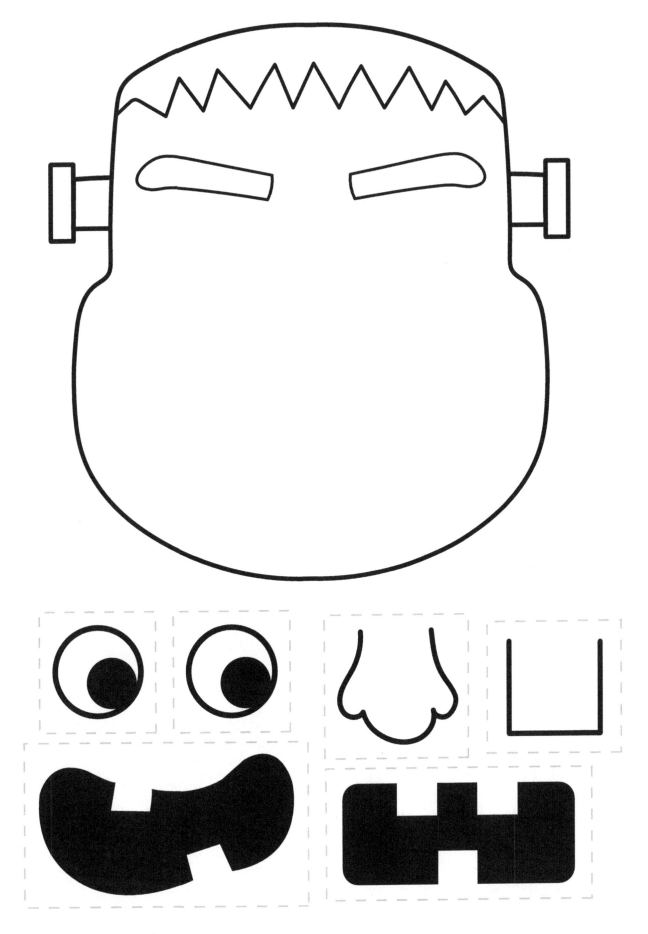

Put the Halloween cat
puzzle back together!

Match the heads to bodies!

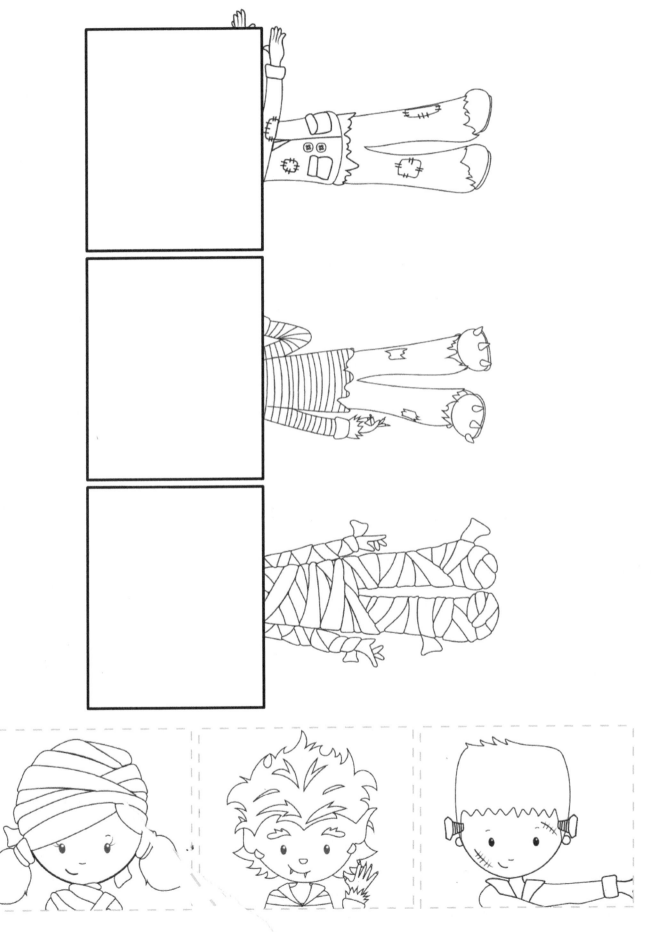

What will the ghost look like?

Put the monsters in the school!

Put a face on the pumpkin!

Put the apples on the tray!

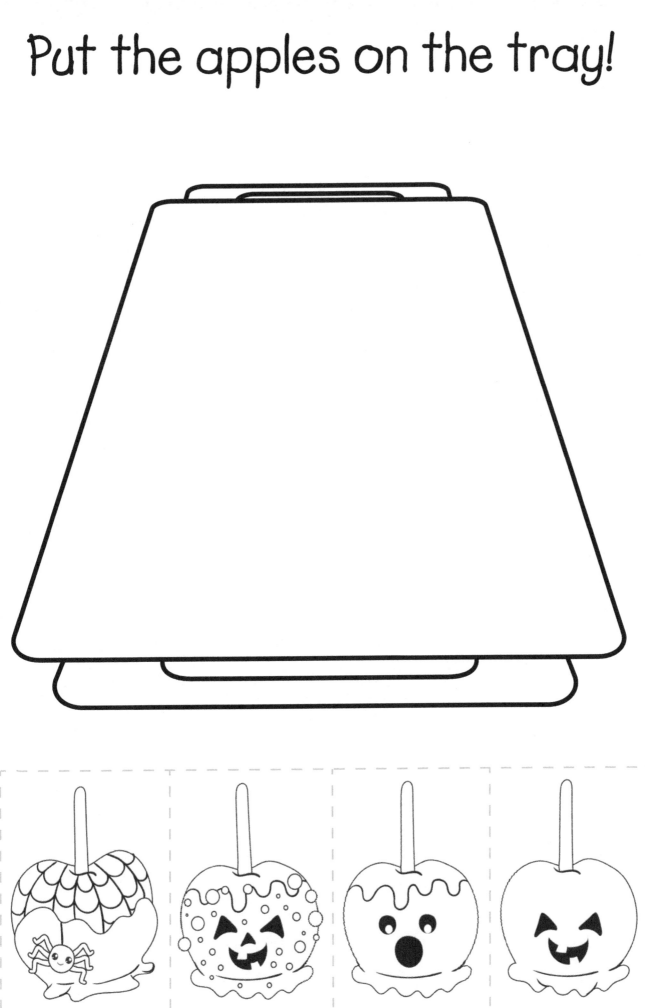

What will the ghost look like?

Put the door and windows on the haunted house!

What will the ghost look like?

Put the bats around the moon!

Put a face on the pumpkin!

Made in the USA
Coppell, TX
22 October 2022

85138851R00037